WHAT ARE YOU
HERE TO
HEAL?

Balboa Press books may be ordered through booksellers or by contacting:

Balboa Press
A Division of Hay House
1663 Liberty Drive
Bloomington, IN 47403
www.balboapress.com
1 (877) 407-4847

Because of the dynamic nature of the Internet, any web addresses or links contained in this book may have changed since publication and may no longer be valid. The views expressed in this work are solely those of the author and do not necessarily reflect the views of the publisher, and the publisher hereby disclaims any responsibility for them.

The author of this book does not dispense medical advice or prescribe the use of any technique as a form of treatment for physical, emotional, or medical problems without the advice of a physician, either directly or indirectly. The intent of the author is only to offer information of a general nature to help you in your quest for emotional and spiritual well-being. In the event you use any of the information in this book for yourself, which is your constitutional right, the author and the publisher assume no responsibility for your actions.

Any people depicted in stock imagery provided by Thinkstock are models,
and such images are being used for illustrative purposes only.
Certain stock imagery © Thinkstock.

ISBN: 978-1-5043-9344-7 (sc)
ISBN: 978-1-5043-9345-4 (e)

Print information available on the last page.

Balboa Press rev. date: 07/09/2020

SELF-REFLECTIVE GUIDE

WHAT ARE YOU HEAR TO HEAL?

To get the most benefit of doing the Self-Reflective Guide, it is really important for you to be honest with yourself. You may be in denial and have defended and deflected for so long you may not not even know what is true for you. Some people have never taken the time to look at themselves and look at how they are doing life. This may be you! You may be spinning for so long that you may think this is your normal. If you have grown up with an alcoholic or workaholic parent, have been neglected, have lost a parent through death, divorce or disaster or you have been sexually, emotionally, psychologically, physically, religiously abused or witnessed someone being sexually, emotionally, psychologically, physically, religiously abused, then you may have been spinning for a long time.

The biggest head banger is when "someone you love hurts someone you love." Just notice. Please don't think that I believe it is your fault that you are spinning. You have learned to cope this way. This is not bad nor wrong. You are not bad nor wrong. I am so glad you were able to find something to hold you. You perhaps have used alcohol, prescription drugs, street drugs, shopping, relationships or gambling. You have had to cope and this is how we human beings often cope when faced with challenges that are beyond our control, especially if the above-mentioned events occurred in your childhood.

Being sick and tired of being sick and tired for a long time is not healthy. We all feel sick and tired of being sick and tired, sometimes. You have learned some ways to cope that are not helpful anymore. This is really good news, even when it may not appear that way. This feeling of being sick and tired of being sick and tired is a signal that you are ready to heal. You are ready or this feeling wouldn't be present to come up to heal. You are ready or you wouldn't be reading this book. This is a journey that you don't have to do alone. It's really important to get out of your head and into your heart. By putting what is in your head on paper, you can look at it, study it, see the patterns and be honest with yourself. Lots of people know things intellectually, however, when you start working with these concepts you will find there is a deeper conversation. I often comment that it goes from intellectually knowing something to a cellular level of knowing something. This is a deeper conversation.

How does the Self-Reflective Guide work? I have listed some prompting questions. Answer the questions and write what comes to mind. I hope you find this helpful in deepening your conversation and gaining insight into your situation. There are questions for each chapter and space to write down what thoughts come to mind. Do not censor yourself. No one is going to see this except you. Let your conscious mind and unconscious mind come out to play. Write everything down, even if it feels funny, is embarrassing or seems insignificant. Get every thought out of your head. Do not deny yourself any healing. There are no new thoughts. We just keep replaying the same old ones in different forms. Notice. This is being totally human. You are not alone. You are normal. There is no thought that someone else has not thought. You are not sick, deviant or weird. Bring to the surface the pain, sadness, insecurities, frailties and pettiness that you have buried, denied or deflected. Don't be afraid of yourself, rather be courageous and tenacious for your healing. Heal the suffering in the world, your world.

CHAPTER 1

Sick and Tired of Being Sick and Tired

1. Are you sick and tried of being sick and tired? _____

2. What is making you feel sick and tired?_____
_____

3. What are you thinking about that keeps you awake or unable to sleep?_____
_____
_____

4. What upsets you?_____
Who do you think upsets you and what do you think they have done?_____
_____
_____
_____

5. Are you doing anything in excess? (ie. texting, calling, on facebook, reminiscing, playing an event over and over in your mind, playing video games, complaining, feeling like you can't seem to get ahead, feeling tired all the time, rushing, speeding, risk taking behavior, or yelling and screaming)_____
_____
_____
_____
_____

6. Are you gambling? It may look different. Are you gambling with your health? Are you doing unsafe activities? Are you doing things that will hurt you? If so what are they?
_____
_____
_____
_____
_____

7. Do you feel stuck, angry, frustrated or confused?_____
_____
_____

8. When do you feel like you have to defend yourself?_____
_____
_____

9. Who do you think makes you feel like you have to defend yourself?_____
_____
_____

10. What do you wish they would do instead?_____
_____
_____

NOTES: _____
_____
_____
_____
_____
_____
_____
_____
_____
_____
_____
_____
_____
_____
_____
_____
_____
_____
_____
_____
_____

CHAPTER 2

Slow Down the Spinning

1. Do you think you are going crazy? _____

2. When are you crazy? _____

3. Who do you think is telling you that you are crazy? _____

4. Why do they think you are crazy?

_____

_____

_____

5. Is your life overwhelming?_____

_____

_____

6. What is overwhelming about your life?_____

_____

_____

7. If you said "everything", just notice and write it all down._____

_____

_____

_____

_____

8. Heighten your awareness. What do you think is keeping you busy and exhausted?

_____

_____

_____

_____

9. Are you competing with anyone? This can look different. What is competing for your time? Who do you think is competing for your time?_____
_____
_____

10. What do you tell yourself? I'm not smart enough? I'm too fat? I'm not pretty enough? I'm not athletic enough? I can't do it? I don't have enough money? You fill in the blank. What do you tell yourself about you? _____

I'm _____

I'm _____

I'm _____

I'm _____

I'm _____

I'm _____

I'm _____

I'll be happy when _____

I'll be happy when _____

I'll be happy when _____

I'll be happy when _____

I'll be happy when _____

Finish the sentence and fill in the blanks as you would for yourself or how you feel about others in that situation:

I was abandoned and this means _____

I am divorced and this means _____

I was conceived before wedlock and this means _____

I was neglected as a child and this means _____

I was raped and this means _____

I was sexually abused by _____ and this means _____

I was _____ and this means _____

I am _____ and this means _____

I am _____ and this means _____

I am _____ and this means _____

I am _____ and this means _____

NOTES: _____

_____

_____

_____

_____

_____

_____

_____

_____

_____

_____

_____

_____

_____

_____

_____

_____

_____

_____

_____

CHAPTER 3

Six Traps of the Ego

TRAP #1 – TRYING TO UNDERSTAND THINGS

1. Where is it that you are stuck trying to figure out something? Why would they say that to me? What were they trying to tell me? Why would they behave so poorly? What are you trying to understand?_____

_____

_____

2. What doesn't make sense to you?_____

_____

_____

3. When are you double dipping? When does it happen that no matter what you do, you can't be happy? When does it happen that not matter what you think, you can't be happy?

_____

_____

_____

TRAP #2 – UNREALISTIC EXPECTATIONS

1. When am I being unrealistic to myself?_____

_____

_____

2. When am I being unrealistic to my partner?_____

_____

_____

CHAPTER 5

The Car of Your Life

1. Who is driving the car of your life: ego, higher self, soul, or highest self? _____

_____

2. Is this who you want driving the car of your life? _____

3. What life do you want to live? _____

_____

_____

4. What wake-up calls have you not listened to? _____

_____

_____

_____

5. When have you not listened to yourself? _____

_____

_____

_____

6. What is your natural addiction of choice: food, sex, safety, power, acceptance, approval, attention, esteem, or status?

_____

_____

7. What is your unnatural addiction of choice: sleeping pills, anxiety medication, pain medication, other pharmaceutical drugs, street drugs, gambling, religion or money? ____

_____

_____

_____

8. How are you numbing your feelings? _____
_____
_____
_____

9. What other things do you use to numb your feelings i.e., urgency, busyness, boredom, workaholism, or shopping?
_____
_____

10. When was the first time you starting numbing your feelings? How old were you? It has been my experience that there is often an event. What happened?
_____
_____
_____

NOTES: _____
_____
_____
_____
_____
_____
_____
_____
_____
_____
_____
_____
_____
_____
_____
_____
_____
_____
_____
_____
_____

CHAPTER 6

The Accordion of Life

1. What is your ego telling you right now? "This is psychobabble." "This is too hard."

_____

_____

2. What is still challenging you?_____

_____

_____

3. How can you meet these challenges differently?_____

_____

_____

4. What can you tell yourself instead? "I've got this." "Things are changing." "I don't have to suffer." "I have a choice." What can you tell yourself that is much more loving to you?

_____

_____

5. What would you tell your best friend that would be encouraging, if your best friend were experiencing the same thing that you have experienced?

_____

_____

_____

NOTES: _____

_____

_____

_____

_____

_____

_____

CHAPTER 7

Being Human

1. What is it about being human that you don't like? _____
_____
_____

2. What frailties do you hide? What don't you want anyone to know about you? _____
_____
_____
_____

3. The ultimate addiction is the addiction to your thinking. What are you thinking over and over again? _____
_____
_____

4. When you are safe and supported. What does it feel like to feel your pain? _____
_____
_____
_____

5. When you are safe and supported. What does it feel like to feel your fear? _____
_____
_____
_____

6. When you are safe and supported. What does it feel like to feel your sadness? _____
_____
_____

7. When you are safe and supported. What does it feel like to feel happiness? _____
_____
_____

8. When you are safe and supported. What do you do when you are uncomfortable? ___

_____

_____

9. When you are safe and supported. What don't you want to deal with in your life? ___

_____

_____

_____

10. When you are safe and supported. What is it that you have come to heal? _____

_____

_____

_____

NOTES: _____

_____

_____

_____

_____

_____

_____

_____

_____

_____

_____

_____

_____

_____

_____

_____

_____

_____

_____

_____

_____

CHAPTER 8

Multigenerational Patterns

1. Have you noticed any patterns in your life? Have you noticed a pattern in your family? It may look different but similar._____

_____

_____

2. What do you want to heal?_____

_____

_____

3. What pattern or thought is running your life? Where did you get this thought?_____

_____

_____

4. What thoughts have you inherited from your your family that you have accepted and made your own?

_____

_____

5. How do you move beyond this pattern?_____

_____

_____

NOTES: _____

_____

_____

_____

_____

_____

_____

_____

CHAPTER 9

The Form is Different but the Content is the Same

1. Where are you suffering?_____
_____
_____

2. What are you role modeling?_____
_____
_____

3. Where do you project your feelings onto someone or something else?_____
_____
_____

4. Where is FEAR: False Evidence Appearing Real in your life? _____
_____
_____

5. Where is FEAR: Feeling Excited And Ready in your life?_____
_____
_____

NOTES: _____
_____
_____
_____
_____
_____
_____
_____
_____
_____
_____

CHAPTER 10

Old Paradigm: War – Divide and Conquer

1. Where are you choosing war rather than peace in your life?_____

_____

_____

2. Where does divide and conquer play out in your life?_____

_____

_____

3. Who are you at war with: ex-partner, employer, parent or children?_____

_____

_____

_____

4. What do you want for your life really: War or Peace?_____

_____

_____

5. When you got into your relationship did you try to help or rescue your partner?_____

_____

_____

6. When do you feel like you are a victim in your relationship? _____

_____

_____

7. Have you ever hurt your partner: emotionally, psychologically, or physically?_____

_____

_____

_____

8. The Drama Triangle, first coined by Stephen Karpman._____
_____
_____

Rescuer

1. Do you do something for someone they can do themselves?
2. Do you do something for someone they haven't asked you to do?
3. Do you put more energy into their problem than they do?
4. Do you realize you don't really want to do what you are doing for them and come to resent them?

_____
_____
_____
_____
_____
_____
_____
_____
_____

Victim

1. What makes you feel like a victim?
2. Who are you with when you feel like a victim?
3. Did either of your parents see themselves as a victim?

_____
_____
_____
_____
_____
_____
_____
_____

Perpetrator

1. Are you criticizing, nagging, blaming, rigid or angry?
2. Who are you angry at?
3. Is there a pattern?

_____
_____
_____
_____
_____
_____
_____
_____
_____
_____

9. What is your go to position: Rescuer, Victim or Perpetrator?
Can you see where you flip back and forth?

_____
_____
_____

10. What is the difference between rescuing and caring? What are some examples in your life?_____

_____
_____

NOTES: _____

_____
_____
_____
_____
_____
_____
_____
_____
_____

CHAPTER 11

New Paradigm: Love - Inclusion and Acceptance

1. Are you Love or Fear?_____
_____
_____

2. Why do you think you are here? _____
_____
_____

3. What is your deeper conversation? _____
_____
_____

4. Do you want the suffering to stop in the world? When you stop the suffering in your life, the world will change. That has been my experience. Give it a try. You have nothing to lose but your suffering.
_____
_____
_____

5. Can you find divinity in all things and in everyone?_____
_____
_____

6. Can you suspend your judgment of someone and just see divinity or compassion?____
_____
_____

7. Are you projecting your fears onto them? Just take a look._____
_____
_____

8. What would happen if we were all one?_____
_____
_____

9. What would happen if you were no longer separate?_____
_____
_____

10. What would living your life from love, peace, trust, wonder, faith, support, balance, patience, tolerance, compassion and forgiveness look like for you?_____
_____
_____
_____

NOTES: _____
_____
_____
_____
_____
_____
_____
_____
_____
_____
_____
_____
_____
_____
_____
_____
_____
_____
_____
_____
_____

CHAPTER 12

Connectedness/Soul

1. Can you relate to our connectedness being analogous to ice cubes?_____

_____

_____

_____

2. Where in your life have you noticed that you are a part of something much greater?__

_____

_____

3. Where have you embraced the unknown or unseen and just trusted?

_____

_____

_____

4. What stuff are you hoping will make you happy?_____

_____

_____

_____

5. If you weren't afraid what would you do?_____

_____

_____

_____

NOTES: _____

_____

_____

_____

_____

_____

CHAPTER 13

Sleep, Nutrition, Exercise, Nature, Meditation, Connectedness

1. Where could you be kinder to yourself?

_____

_____

_____

2. SLEEP

Are you getting enough sleep? There are three kinds of not sleeping:

a) Are you able to fall asleep?_____

b) Are you able to stay asleep?_____

c) Do you wake up early and can't return to sleep? _____

3. NUTRITION

What can you do to improve your nutrition?_____

a) Are you eating regularly, especially starting with a breakfast?_____

b) Are you eating fresh, raw or whole foods?_____

c) Are you eating a lot of processed food – anything in a box or jar? _____

3. EXERCISE

a) Are you getting regular exercise? _____

b) What can you start doing differently today?_____

c) What can you do that would help you maintain your exercise program? ____

4. NATURE

How can you get nature into your life?_____

a) Are there any nature walks or parks near you?_____

b) Are there any bodies of water, streams or ravines near you?_____

c) Are there any nature clubs or wildlife conservations areas near you? _____

5. MEDITATION AND RELAXATION

What can you do to meditate or relax more? Are there any meditation or Tai Chi groups in your area? What do you find relaxing?

_____

6. BUILD HEALTHY CONNECTIONS

What interests do you have that you can share?_____

Who are the healthy people in your life?_____

Write an example of when you have had goose bumps or chills. What was happening at the time? Do more of what makes you happy and gives you goose bumps._____

_____

NOTES: _____

_____

_____

_____

_____

_____

_____

_____

_____

_____

_____

_____

_____

_____

_____

_____

_____

_____

_____

_____

_____

_____

_____

_____

_____

_____

_____

_____

CHAPTER 14

Nightmares

1. Briefly, write down your nightmares._____
_____
_____

2. Before you go to sleep, ask your nightmares what they are trying to tell you. It may take a few tries, as it sounds a little far-fetched. Your rational mind may not think it will work. Give it a try. What have you got to lose? Write your experience._____
_____
_____
_____

3. What do you think your nightmare wants to tell you?_____
_____
_____

4. How is your stress coming out "sideways"?_____
_____
_____
_____

5. How is your body telling you something is wrong?_____
_____
_____

NOTES: _____
_____
_____
_____
_____
_____
_____

CHAPTER 15

What Love is and What Love Isn't

1. Are you confused about love? What do you think love is?_____
_____
_____

2. What kind of love do you want to experience: Love of the soul, Love of the body, Love of the child, Longstanding Love, Love of the mind, Playful Love, or Love of Self?
_____
_____
_____

3. If you loved yourself, what would it look like?_____
_____
_____

NOTES: _____
_____
_____
_____
_____
_____
_____
_____
_____
_____
_____
_____
_____
_____
_____
_____

Chapter 16

What is a Healthy Relationship?

1. Have you thought about whether your relationship is healthy or not?_____
_____
_____
_____

2. What is right in your relationship and what is wrong in your relationship? _____
_____
_____

3. Can you relate to the movie example?_____
_____
_____
_____

4. In your relationship, do you feel like you can't do anything right, that you are saying things to keep the peace and avoid an argument, or feeling that nothing ever gets resolved. Is your partner jealous, a poor sport, know-it-all, or blames you or others for their problems?
_____
_____

5. What kind of relationship do you want to have with yourself and others? _____
_____
_____
_____

NOTES: _____
_____
_____
_____
_____
_____

Chapter 17

Forgiveness

1. What were you told about forgiveness?_____
_____
_____

2. Can you replace understanding for your hurt?_____
_____
_____

3. Where could it fit for you?_____
_____
_____

4. Who do you think hurt you?_____
_____
_____

5. Are you able to see that they don't think like you think?_____
_____
_____

6. What do you believe they would have to think to do what they did to you?_____
_____
_____

7. Can you be open to consider, they are lying to themselves? How do you think that must feel inside for them to lie and deny themselves who they really are?_____
_____
_____
_____

8. What would your highest self do?_____
_____
_____

9. Can you not be defined by what happened to you?_____
_____
_____

10. Can you be defined by your true nature?_____
_____
_____

NOTES: _____
_____
_____
_____
_____
_____
_____
_____
_____
_____
_____
_____
_____
_____
_____
_____
_____
_____
_____
_____
_____
_____

CHAPTER 18

Shift Happens

1. One thought can keep you in an abusive relationship._____

_____

_____

_____

_____

_____

_____

What one thought is stopping you from your heart's desire?

_____

_____

_____

_____

_____

_____

_____

2. Let the tears wash your heart. When have you wanted to cry and couldn't?_____

_____

_____

_____

_____

_____

_____

3. Whatever shows up, love that. If you can't change it, can you look at it differently?_

_____
_____
_____
_____
_____
_____

4. Love is the answer to every question.

_____
_____
_____
_____
_____
_____

5. It's coming up to heal. Don't be afraid of your feelings.

_____
_____
_____
_____
_____
_____

6. You are never upset for the reason you think or say. What are you reliving from your past? _____

_____
_____
_____
_____
_____
_____

7. When you give someone advice, know that the advice is actually for you. What advice do you give other people?_____

_____

_____

_____

_____

_____

_____

8. As soon as you defend yourself, you are going to war. Who are you at war with? (Mother, Father, Sister, Brother, Employer, Ex-partner, Friend, Co-worker)

_____

_____

_____

_____

_____

_____

9. You don't get to talk to me that way. You can set a firm boundary. Try it. How did it work?_____

_____

_____

_____

_____

_____

_____

10. Stop using other people to beat yourself up. Where are you using other people to beat yourself up?_____

_____

_____

_____

_____

_____

_____

11. Keep myself small and suffering. When are you feeling small and suffering?

_____
_____
_____
_____
_____
_____

12. Just notice. What are you noticing?_____
_____
_____
_____
_____
_____
_____

13. You can choose to suffer or not. You can't change the situation, however, you can change what you make it mean._____
_____
_____
_____
_____
_____
_____

14. Exercise discernment. What does that mean for you?_____
_____
_____
_____
_____
_____
_____

15. What you resist, persists. What is persisting in your life? _____

_____

_____

_____

_____

_____

_____

16. You do until you don't. Keep practicing. What have you noticed?

_____

_____

_____

_____

_____

_____

_____

17. The universe will give you lots of practice. _____

_____

_____

_____

_____

_____

_____

_____

18. Be prepared to be wrong. How can this statement be freeing to you?

_____

_____

_____

_____

_____

_____

_____

19. Could they be right? Provide yourself a moment to feel this phrase. What are you feeling?_____

_____

_____

_____

_____

_____

20. You are living in a world that doesn't exist yet._____

_____

_____

_____

_____

_____

21. Clean up your mess. What messes do you have to clean up?_____

_____

_____

_____

_____

_____

22. Don't jump into their nightmare._____

_____

_____

_____

_____

_____

23. All behavior is purposeful. What is the purpose of your behavior, especially when you are spinning or sick and tired of being sick and tired?_____

_____

_____

_____

_____

_____

_____

24. The form is different but the content is the same. What forms of the same pattern have you noticed?_____

_____

_____

_____

_____

_____

_____

_____

25. You're allowed to ask for what you need. Where have you felt shut down, not heard and that your opinion doesn't matter?_____

_____

_____

_____

_____

_____

_____

26. We sell out on ourselves for the love, approval and appreciation of others. What have you done to get what you want?_____

_____

_____

_____

_____

_____

_____

27. It is never wrong to love someone. Who do you still care about even though most people think you're crazy?_____

_____

_____

_____

_____

_____

28. The better you do, the better your children will do. If your children are acting out or not doing well, look to see where you are not doing well._____

_____

_____

_____

_____

_____

_____

29. Your feelings are your way out of suffering. When I ask people what they are feeling they often don't know. What are you feeling right now, write it down._____

_____

_____

_____

_____

_____

30. I'm not my story. What was your story?_____

_____

_____

_____

_____

_____

31. There is no "out there"; there is only "in here." What are you projecting?

_____

_____

_____

_____

_____

_____

32. You are the only one you can change. What are you hoping will change?_____

_____

_____

_____

_____

_____

_____

33. Hurt people hurt people. Who do you think hurt you? Who do you think you are hurting?_____

_____

_____

_____

_____

_____

_____

34. Bad neighborhood. Take a right. What neighborhood are you in this moment? Is it peaceful and loving or is it stressful and anxiety provoking?_____

_____

_____

_____

_____

_____

35. It's like drinking poison expecting them to die. What poisonous thoughts have you been thinking?_____

_____

_____

_____

_____

_____

36. Choose life not death. What suffering thoughts are coming up for you?_____

_____

_____

_____

_____

_____

_____

37. Life is all about death. Where do you not want to change?_____

_____

_____

_____

_____

_____

38. I would do those things too if I believed what they believed. Where are you expecting people to believe what you believe?_____

_____

_____

_____

_____

39. If you are suffering, you are choosing pain over peace. When are you choosing pain over peace? Where are you choosing activities that are unhealthy or destructive? What comes to mind?_____

_____

_____

_____

_____

_____

_____

40. Everything you want from others, you can give to yourself. What do you want from someone? Is it love, approval, acceptance, money, to be admired, to be appreciated or to be trusted?_____

_____

_____

_____

_____

_____

_____

_____

41. It only takes one to heal and that one is you._____

_____

_____

_____

_____

_____

_____

42. It's a deeper conversation. What are the deeper conversations that you are noticing?

_____

_____

_____

_____

_____

_____

43. You are loved much more than you know. It's important to remind yourself that you are loved. Who loves you?_____

_____

_____

_____

_____

_____

44. Your peace is a thought away. What thoughts take away your peace?_____

_____

_____

_____

_____

_____

45. Your power lies in your choices. What are the choices that you like?_____

_____

_____

_____

_____

_____

46. It's not good or bad. Without judgment, notice how you feel about things._____

_____

_____

_____

_____

47. Loving yourself: what would that look like? How do you love yourself?_____

_____

_____

_____

_____

_____

_____

48. You matter. Do you feel that you matter?_____

_____

_____

_____

_____

_____

_____

49. Working it out. Where are things not getting resolved?_____

_____

_____

_____

_____

_____

_____

50. There is no time, only the present. When are you not present?_____

_____

_____

_____

_____

_____

_____

51. What you are holding on to isn't worth holding on to. What do you need to let go of?_____

_____

_____

_____

_____

_____

52. Take the high road because all other roads lead nowhere. What dilemma are you facing?_____

_____

_____

_____

_____

_____

_____

53. Fantasy Land is a great place to visit. I don't recommend you hang out there for long periods of time. What fantasies do you have about the person you think hurt you?

_____

_____

_____

_____

_____

54. Not giving in, not giving up, rather standing in your truth. What is your truth?

_____

_____

_____

_____

_____

55. What does that look like? What patterns are you noticing?_____

_____

_____

_____

_____

_____

_____

56. Doing it differently. What do you need to do differently?_____

_____

_____

_____

_____

_____

_____

57. There is nothing to forgive._____

_____

_____

_____

_____

_____

_____

58. What have you noticed that makes you shift?_____

_____

_____

_____

_____

_____

_____

59. Make a shift up for yourself. _____

_____

_____

_____

_____

_____

60. Trust your journey. _____

_____

_____

_____

_____

_____

_____

What would it look like if you trusted your journey? _____

_____

_____

_____

_____

_____

What are your favourite shifts? _____

_____

_____

_____

_____

_____

_____

What other shifts have you noticed?_____
_____
_____
_____
_____
_____

What helps you shift?_____
_____
_____
_____
_____
_____
_____

I hope you have found the self-reflective guide truly helpful. In summary, it is important to find out what works for you. These are shifts that I work with regularly with clients and in my own life to remain present and conscious. With **practice** you will be surprised at how quickly they work into discussion and action in your world. Remember the universe is going to give you lots of situations and time to practice. If you miss an opportunity it will present itself again, especially if you are looking for it. Don't forget to have fun. This may seem like a lot of work or very overwhelming. Just notice that that thought will keep you suffering. You can only really do one thing at a time. So just do one thing at a time. Don't worry the same issue will come up over and over again in different forms until you heal it. That is what you have come here to heal, so it is going to come again and again. This is really very good news. You probably never looked at it like this before, however, you are here to heal all the suffering in your world. It starts with you and your world.

Love is the answer to every question. This is my love letter to you. Love has so many forms. Love can seem so confusing, however, now you have discernment and some help. Did you catch the ego trap, confusion? It's very exciting to see the many forms of love. Love can look like compassion for yourself and others, it can look like cookies, it can look like silence, it can look like a book, it can look like volunteer work, it can look like a hug, it can look like washing a car or the dishes, it can look like a phone call, it can look like making amends, it can look like saying no, it can look like asking for what you need, it can look like standing in your truth and it can look like the expression of your true self. The form is different but the content is the same. Almost anything can be loving. I didn't think so at that time. I was shocked when my job was eliminated. I loved what I was doing. It made my choice to finish my book very easy. I had been working on it for a while. I was able to shift to see that the universe had something different and perhaps even better for me. I choose life. I have learned to trust my journey even when it's not what I think I want.

Wow. This is where my power lies in my choices. You don't get to choose what happens rather, you get to choose what you make it mean. I would encourage you to choose love every time. Love is the answer to every question.

So there you have it. My banquet of ideas, suggestions and experience served with compassion, support and of course love. It is important to seek meaning not power. Try them out and see what works for you.

In conclusion, you are not your body; you have a body. You are not your thoughts; you are the one listening to your thoughts. You get to choose your thoughts. You get to choose if you are going to listen to your ego or your highest self. You are here to express the highest form of yourself. When you don't express the highest form of yourself you are living a lie and that doesn't feel very good. Love is the highest expression of your true self. You have forgotten who you are. You are a spiritual being having a human experience to express your divinity and to heal your mind and your perceived separation from divinity. Everything is divine. Bring your microscope and see what has always been here: love.

There is no time. I am so comforted by this statement. There is no time. Feel that. You are in the perfect place. Where you are right now. The past is over, gone, non existent. Not in the way that it doesn't matter or didn't happen; rather, in a way that it doesn't get to define you. The only time there is, is now. You! Reading this book. Now you get to define you in this moment. Who do you want to be in this moment? Do you want to be spinning, sick and tired of being sick and tired, racing from place to place or person to person? This is war. This is war with who you really are. Do you want to be a body, only thinking of the material, safety, survival or the mind that creates and chooses your divinity, your highest self and trust the wonder that created you? You get to decide. The choice is yours. End the suffering in the world, your world, in this moment and this moment and this moment. Start with you and your world will change. Love is the highest expression of yourself and your true identity. You are love in human form. Love is the answer to every question.

NOTES: _____

Printed in the United States
By Bookmasters